RIVER and CANAL

written and illustrated by

EDWARD BOYER

THE POCOSINK NAVIGATION CO.

OHIOPOLIS AQUEDUCT

AD. 1848

WITHDRAWN

Holiday House / New York

For my father, who knows how everything works.

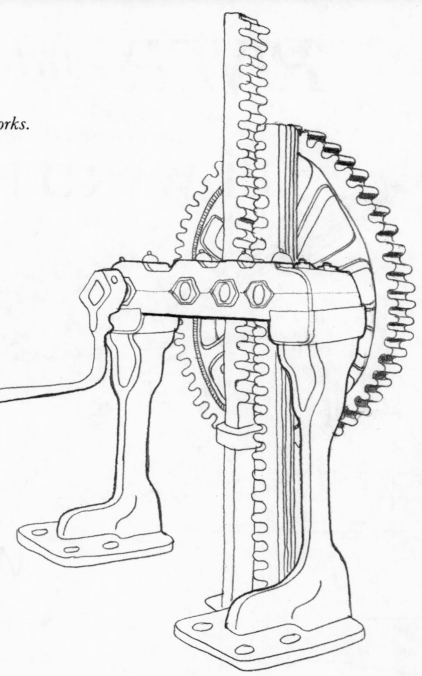

Copyright © 1986 by Edward Boyer
All rights reserved
Printed in the United States of America
First Edition

Library of Congress Cataloging in Publication Data

River and canal.

Includes index.
SUMMARY: Describes the designing, construction, and
operation of an imaginary nineteenth-century canal,
based upon similar histories of real canals.
   1. Canals—Design and construction—Juvenile
literature. 2. River engineering—Juvenile literature.
3. Hydraulic structures—Design and construction—
Juvenile literature. 4. Inland navigation—Juvenile
literature. [1. Canals] I. Title.
TC745.B69   1986   627′.13   85-21900
ISBN 0-8234-0598-2

The Pocosink Canal is imaginary, as is the Pocosink Navigation Company. The story of its design, construction, and operation is based upon similar histories of real canals. The technology used on the Pocosink is taken from several different canals of the same period.

The traces and remains of early-nineteenth century canals can be found across North America, east of the Mississippi River. Most of the waterways lie in ruins today. To find them you must leave the road, cross the railroad tracks, and approach the river, which was the first highway on the continent. There, near the river whose course it usually followed, is what remains of the canal.

Some canals did not follow rivers. The Erie Canal was built from the city of Albany, on the Hudson River, to the city of Buffalo, on Lake Erie; of its 363 miles across New York State, only 110 miles followed a river, the Mohawk. Other canals were dug across land to connect natural waterways.

But most canals followed river valleys because rivers, in their ancient courses, offered the easiest route from the land's interior to its coast. The canal made rivers more navigable for the purposes of a growing commerce.

The early canals were enormous works that took a huge investment of wealth, labor, and invention. The canals were built by people who used the materials and skills at hand to supply the needs they faced. The story of the Pocosink Canal is a story of work on land and river—work that used the land's resources and followed the river's course and changed the landscape forever.

E. BOYER
April 1985

The land that faced European settlers as they came to North America was a mostly low, green coastline indented by many bays, inlets, and rivers. Rivers flowed over many rapids and waterfalls on their course from the mountains far inland to the ocean. Ships that sailed up the rivers from the sea were stopped by the first rapids they encountered. At these places, port cities developed where ships were unloaded and goods traded. Goods sent farther inland were put on mules or in wagons. The position of the falls or rapids on a map of the coast was called the fall line; it was the first obstacle to inland travel.

The land's first people traveled easily on its rivers and lakes. The Indians built canoes of wood and bark to carry goods and war parties. If they came to a place where rapids blocked their way, they carried goods and canoes around the obstacle. The French traders called these carrying places "portages."

European farmers and merchants could not use small, fragile canoes for their cargo. Their animals, furniture, iron, and sacks of grain were too heavy, so they carried them in large wooden boats. Because their boats could not pass above the rapids, most settlers spread out along the coast, no farther upriver than the fall line, and trade between settlements was carried by small coastal ships.

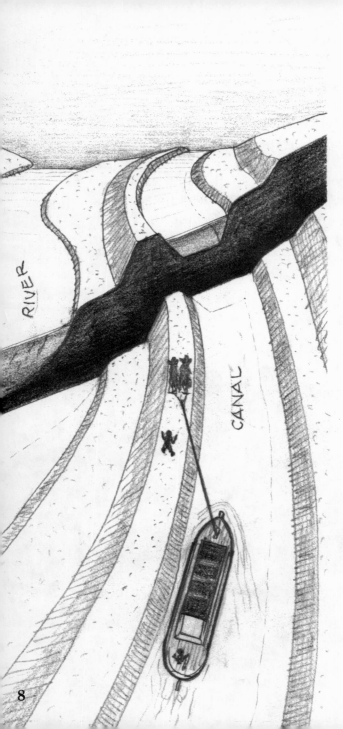

RIVER

CANAL

When the coastal lands filled up and settlers moved inland, the problems of transportation became serious. Inland farmers who were pushing the frontier beyond the mountains wanted to buy cloth, stoves, and hardware from the coastal cities. They had to sell their grain and other produce to pay for such things. The cost of hauling goods in wagons was so great that the inland settlers couldn't afford to either buy or sell; the cost of transportation was several times the value of the freight. Inland travel by boat was blocked by rapids and shallows on the rivers.

Canals were the answer. With a canal, the swift waters of a river could be held behind dams and led into quiet channels. Then heavy boats could move easily both upstream and down. Such a canal would ease the movement of freight, making trade between inland and coastal cities flourish.

Canals had been used in Europe for many years; they were the easiest and cheapest means of shipping goods. During the period from 1790 to 1830, canal schemes were proposed for nearly every river in eastern North America. During the twenty years from 1815 to 1835, more than 3,000 miles of canals were built. State and national governments and private companies all promoted ambitious canal schemes. About half of them were completed.

One of the private companies that took part in the canal boom was the Pocosink Navigation Company. The company proposed to make the Pocosink River navigable with dams and canals. The canal was the idea of Ezra Horne, an inventor and self-taught engineer, and his partner, Joshua Warren, a surveyor. The two men traveled the course of the eastward-flowing Pocosink River to its source, where a portage to the westward-flowing Bleak River gave access to the Ohio Valley and the interior of the continent. They would build a canal along the Pocosink and join it to the Bleak River so that boats could travel to the western settlements.

The partners needed money to build the canal, so they formed the Pocosink Navigation Company and sold shares to rich merchants and bankers. The buyers of the shares would own a part of the company in proportion to the number of shares they held. The company would pay them a share of the profits earned from fees paid by users of the canal. The stock owners hoped to get a good profit from their investment when the canal was completed.

The partners needed permission from the state government to build the canal. Because the canal would change the river, which belonged to all the people, and because the canal would cross lands belonging to many settlers who lived near the river, the project needed the consent of the legislature. This consent was written in a document called "A Charter for the Improvement of Navigation on the Pocosink and Bleak Rivers in the State of Columbia; Granted at the Capital A.D. 1817, and of Independence the 51st Year."

The charter was as wordy as its title; it granted the company the sole right to build and operate a canal, and to use the waters of the Pocosink and Bleak rivers for that purpose. The charter allowed the company to collect fees, or tolls, from those who would use the canal for transportation, and from those who would use the flow in the canal to turn their waterwheels. The state granted these valuable privileges on condition that the canal be maintained for the use of all who would travel or ship goods on it.

Now that Horne and Warren had a charter from the state, and money from the stockholders, they could make a detailed survey of the canal. The partners started from the city of Columbia, where the canal would begin, and moved up the Pocosink Valley. With compass and plane table they plotted the river's course. With chains they measured distances, and with level and rod they tried the river's depth. They used a barometer to measure the river's height above sea level.

The survey took most of the summer to complete. When Horne and Warren reached the highest point near the source of the Pocosink, they crossed the mountain to the source of the Bleak River and continued the survey down that river to the place where it flowed into the great inland river, the Ohio. They would build the canal along the course they surveyed, and join the coast to the Ohio River Valley.

9

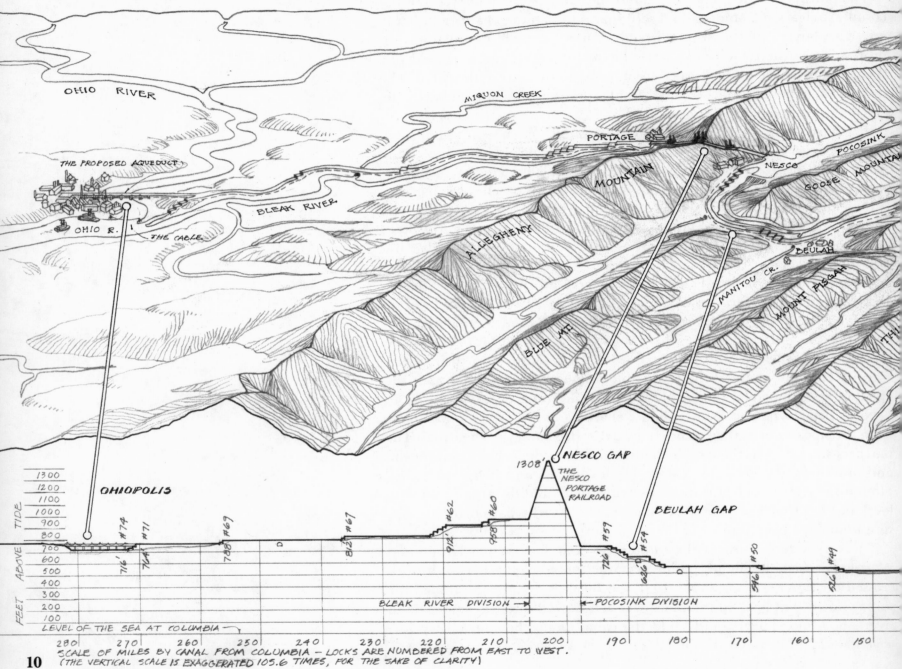

OHIO RIVER

MIQUON CREEK

POCOSINK

PORTAGE

NESCO

MOUNTAIN

GOOSE MOUNTAIN

THE PROPOSED AQUEDUCT

BLEAK RIVER

ALLEGHENY

OHIO R.

THE CABLE

MANITOU CR.

BEULAH

BLUE MT.

MOUNT PISGAH

NESCO GAP

1308'

THE NESCO PORTAGE RAILROAD

BEULAH GAP

OHIOPOLIS

1300
1200
1100
1000
900
800
700
600
500
400
300
200
100

FEET ABOVE TIDE

LEVEL OF THE SEA AT COLUMBIA

#74 #71   716' 704'   788' #69

#67   812'

#62 912'   #60 958'

#59 716'   #54 626'

#50 546'

#49 526'

BLEAK RIVER DIVISION →   ← POCOSINK DIVISION

280   270   260   250   240   230   220   210   200   190   180   170   160   150

SCALE OF MILES BY CANAL FROM COLUMBIA — LOCKS ARE NUMBERED FROM EAST TO WEST.
(THE VERTICAL SCALE IS EXAGGERATED 105.6 TIMES, FOR THE SAKE OF CLARITY)

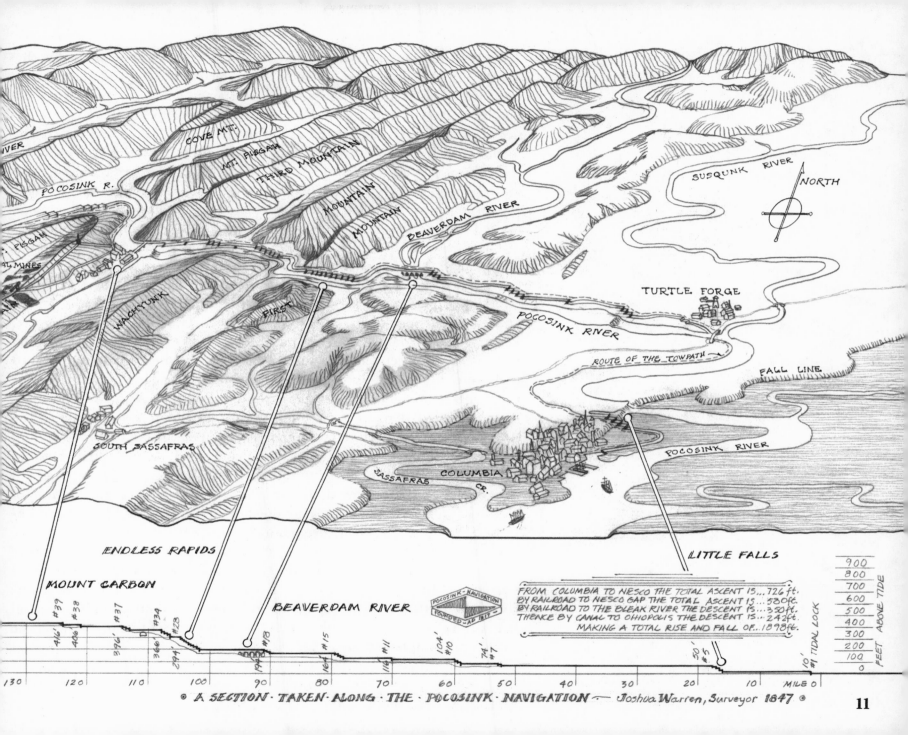

COVE MT.

MT. PISGAH

THIRD MOUNTAIN

MOUNTAIN

MOUNTAIN

MOUNTAIN

POCOSINK R.

BEAVERDAM RIVER

SUSQUNK RIVER

NORTH

. PISGAH

L MINES

TURTLE FORGE

WACHSUNK

FIRST

POCOSINK RIVER

ROUTE OF THE TOWPATH

FALL LINE

SOUTH SASSAFRAS

COLUMBIA

POCOSINK RIVER

SASSAFRAS CR.

ENDLESS RAPIDS

LITTLE FALLS

MOUNT CARBON

BEAVERDAM RIVER

POCOSINK · NAVIGATION
FOUNDED ~AD 1817

FROM COLUMBIA TO NESCO THE TOTAL ASCENT IS...726 ft.
BY RAILROAD TO NESCO GAP THE TOTAL ASCENT IS...580 ft.
BY RAILROAD TO THE BLEAK RIVER THE DESCENT IS...350 ft.
THENCE BY CANAL TO OHIOPOLIS THE DESCENT IS...242 ft.
MAKING A TOTAL RISE AND FALL OF...1898 ft.

900
800
700
600
500
400
300
200
100
0

FEET ABOVE TIDE

#39 #38 #37 #34 #28 #18 #15 #11 #10 #7 #5 #1 TIDAL LOCK

416' 406' 396' 366' 294' 194' 164' 116' 104' 74' 50' 10'

130   120   110   100   90   80   70   60   50   40   30   20   10   MILE 0

⊛ A SECTION · TAKEN · ALONG · THE · POCOSINK · NAVIGATION — Joshua Warren, Surveyor 1847 ⊛

11

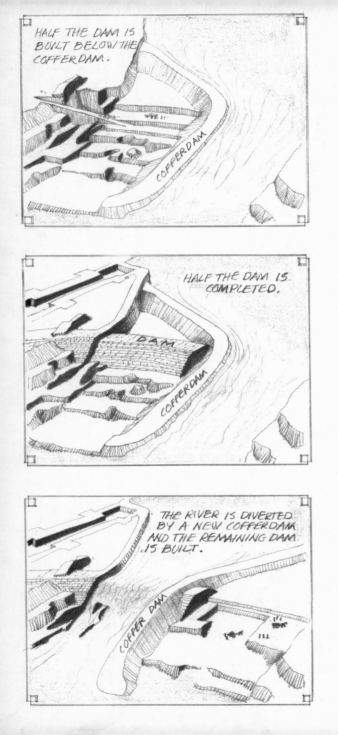

HALF THE DAM IS BUILT BELOW THE COFFERDAM.

COFFERDAM

HALF THE DAM IS COMPLETED.

DAM

COFFERDAM

THE RIVER IS DIVERTED BY A NEW COFFERDAM AND THE REMAINING DAM IS BUILT.

COFFERDAM

By 1818 Horne and Warren had completed their survey; plans for the canal were in a final state. As soon as winter released its icy hold on the river, work began. In March, Horne and Warren led a crew of eighty men 7 miles upstream from Columbia, where the Pocosink tumbled over a series of rapids called the Little Falls of the Pocosink. This was the first obstacle on the river, and here the partners would build a dam to make the river above the falls navigable. Below the falls would be a canal along the south bank of the river, all the way to Columbia. The canal would be filled with water from the dam. Horne calculated that a dam 26 feet high was needed to raise the water above the falls and fill the canal.

They set to work building a temporary dam, or cofferdam, above the place where the permanent dam would be. The cofferdam was built from the south bank by sinking wooden cages filled with rocks into the swift river. The cofferdam grew slowly as men and mules hauled timber, rocks, and earth to stop the river's flow and direct it toward the north bank. When the cofferdam was about halfway across the river, it was extended downstream to keep the water away from the exposed riverbed. Soil and rock were dug from the riverbed with shovels and picks. Gunpowder was used to blast boulders and bedrock; a level, solid base for the dam was ready. Large, flat rocks dug from a quarry upstream were floated to the damsite on rafts and placed with their long dimensions pointing upstream.

When half the dam was finished, the cofferdam was removed. Another cofferdam was built from the north bank to divert the river from the site of the remaining half of the dam. Since it was midsummer, the volume of water was a fraction of the spring flow; otherwise it would have been impossible to direct the river through a channel half its normal width.

Completion of the permanent dam allowed the workmen to take away all of the cofferdam and admire the result of their efforts, the first artificial barrier on the Pocosink River. This barrier would raise the level of the river behind it, making it navigable for miles. It would also fill the canal between Little Falls and Columbia. The men next set to work digging the canal and completing the locks.

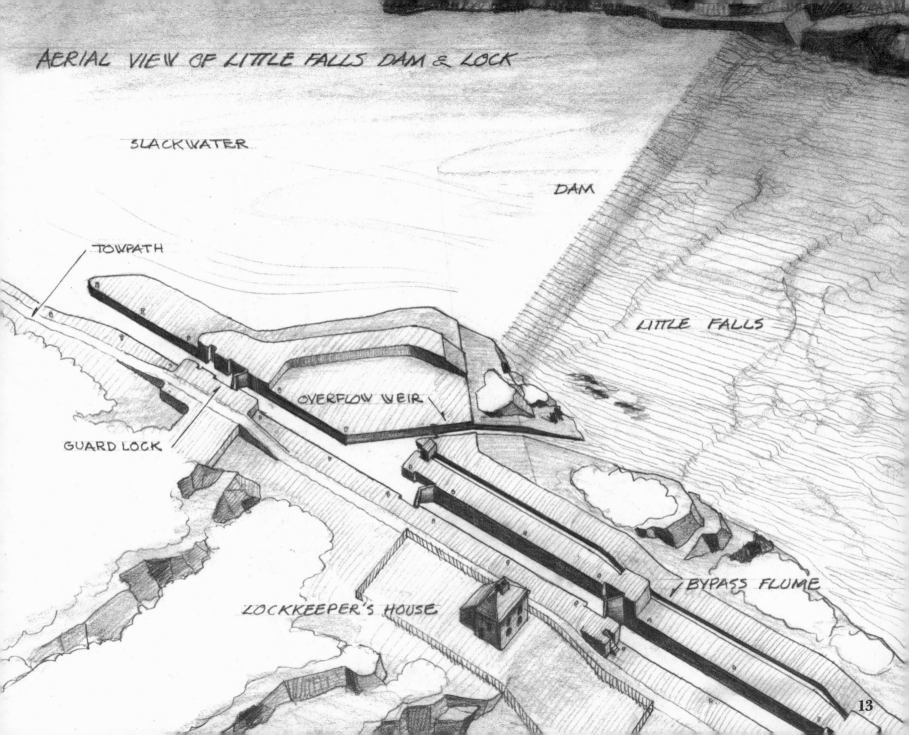

AERIAL VIEW OF LITTLE FALLS DAM & LOCK

SLACKWATER

DAM

TOWPATH

LITTLE FALLS

OVERFLOW WEIR

GUARD LOCK

BYPASS FLUME

LOCKKEEPER'S HOUSE

13

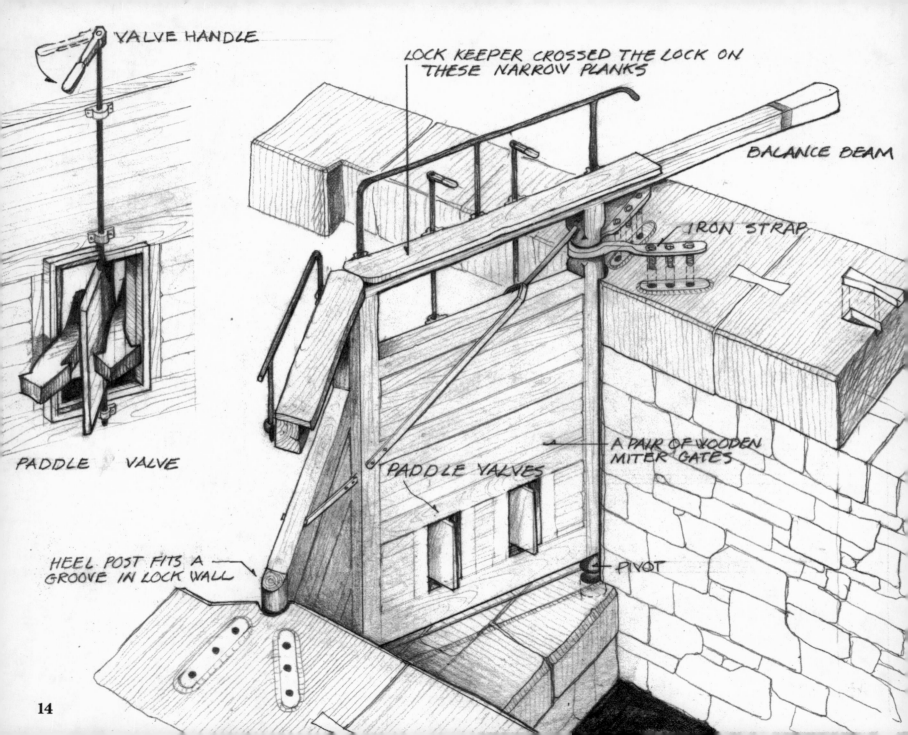

VALVE HANDLE

PADDLE VALVE

LOCK KEEPER CROSSED THE LOCK ON THESE NARROW PLANKS

BALANCE BEAM

IRON STRAP

A PAIR OF WOODEN MITER GATES

PADDLE VALVES

PIVOT

HEEL POST FITS A GROOVE IN LOCK WALL

WATER PRESSURE

MITER

THE HEEL POST IS HELD TIGHT AGAINST THE LOCK WALL BY WATER PRESSURE

Locks are watery stairs that enable boats to move from one level to another. At Little Falls, they would move boats from the water level below the falls to that above the falls. Locks work like giant bathtubs with watertight doors at each end to admit boats. When the doors are closed, the lock is filled with water to lift the boat, or it can be emptied to lower the boat. The locks can lift a boat to great heights where they are connected in a series. A series of locks is called a flight, just as a series of steps is called a flight of stairs.

The locks at Little Falls were built in a flight of four. Each lock would raise the water level 10 feet, for a total lift of 40 feet from the canal level at Columbia to the height of the water behind Little Falls dam.

The lock's doors are called miter gates because they meet at an angle. The edges are mitered, or perfectly angled, where they meet to make a tight fit. The gates swing open toward the upstream end of the lock; when they are closed, the pressure of the water pushes the mitered edges tightly together. The greater the pressure, the more tightly the gates are held closed. The gates turn on a pivot at the bottom of a heel post and are held in place by iron straps at the top. Paddlelike valves in the miter gates are closed when the lock is filled with water, and opened when the lock is drained.

Opening and closing the gates, directing boats through the locks, and collecting tolls are the job of a lockkeeper and his assistant. Horne had a stone lockkeeper's house built opposite the uppermost lock at Little Falls.

The locks were 12 feet wide and 100 feet long. They held 6 feet of water when emptied to their lowest water level; when filled, they held about 16 feet of water. Built of carefully cut and fitted stones, the sides and bottoms were sealed with cement or clay to prevent leaks.

A small channel called a bypass flume was built between the upper and lower canal sections. The bypass flume would supply the canal below the locks with water when the locks were not being used.

15

Below Little Falls, crews worked on the canal. They dug the canal ditch several feet above the level of the river. Although the Pocosink Canal would follow the river for most of its length, it was built above the level reached by the worst flood anyone could remember; such a location should protect the canal from damage when the river rose.

The canal was 45 feet wide at water level and 6 feet deep; its banks were protected from waves by a curb of stones. On one bank was a towpath where mules would pull boats along the canal.

Water was let into the canal from the river behind the Little Falls dam. The Pocosink River fluctuates widely in the amount and depth of water it carries. Springtime runoff is many times greater than the shallow flow of midsummer, yet flow in a canal has to be fairly constant. Horne estimated the water level at Little Falls for the time of lowest flow and set the level in the canal accordingly. Most of the river's flow went over the dam, and the extra water that entered the canal during seasons of high water was let off through an adjustable gate called a weir. Winter floods were kept out of the canal by heavy miter gates near the canal entrance. These guard locks were normally open, but could be shut during floods to keep debris and water from damaging the canal and locks.

A lock was built where the canal entered the river at Columbia. There its purpose was to adjust the water level in the canal to the river. The river reaches sea level at Columbia; it rises and falls twice a day according to the tidal changes in the ocean. The tidal lock allowed boats to pass into the river no matter what its tide level.

The spring of 1819 brought a flood that nearly wrecked the guard locks at Little Falls; the heavy gates were badly damaged. The canal builders provided for the emergency by cutting grooves in the stone walls of the lock just upstream from the gates. Timbers that fit into the grooves were kept on hand; iron plates bolted to them made them sink as the workers pushed them one after another into the grooves and made a temporary barrier. The stop timbers held water back while the workers drained the lock and repaired the gates.

Repairs delayed the opening of the first section of the Pocosink Canal until late April 1819. The inaugural boat was crowded with a boisterous party of stockholders and city officials. The boat entered the lowest of the Little Falls locks. The gates were closed behind it, and the lockkeeper opened the paddle valves to let water fill the lock. When water rose 10 feet to the level of the next lock, the gates between them were swung open. The lockkeeper pushed on the balance beam that served as a long lever to move the gate.

The boat was towed by hand into the second lock; gates were shut behind it, and the procedure was repeated in each lock until the boat was lifted to the highest level, 40 feet above where it entered the locks.

Descending boats would enter the upper lock; gates would be closed behind it and the lock drained to lower the boat 10 feet to the level of the next lock. The procedure of lowering the boat would be repeated through all four locks until it reached the bottom of the flight.

The boatload of local celebrities was hitched to its mule team and towed out of the lock, into the still water behind the Little Falls dam. The pool extended upriver 22 miles. Rather than dig 22 miles of canal, Horne and Warren used the impounded river as a slack-water navigation, and built a towpath along the cleared bank of the Pocosink.

Slack-water navigation was the purpose of the whole canal. A canal was a ditch filled with still water so that boats could easily navigate up or down it. A river could also serve the purpose where it was stopped by a dam. Where flow in the pool behind a dam was slower than 2 miles per hour, the river channel might be navigated.

At Turtle Forge, near the upper end of slack-water navigation by river, the officials stepped ashore to greet a crowd of grinning spectators. Everyone was treated to sandwiches and lemonade and to the long-winded speechifying that was the favorite entertainment of the age. Both stock owners and townspeople shared a confident hope that the new canal would bring them prosperity.

The day after the ceremonies at Turtle Forge, Horne and Warren went upriver to oversee work on the next canal section. Work crews were already busy at the remote sites; they had become experienced canal builders and could work without much direction from the partners. They had cleared most of the route for the season's construction.

Warren worked in the clearings to mark out the location of locks and the position and depth of excavations. The canal builders worked with hand tools, and with the help of animals they moved heavy carts loaded with earth or sleds loaded with building stone. Trees were cut down to provide materials for lock gates. Everything but ironwork, such as bolts, hinges, and other hardware, was supplied by the land along the canal route.

Where the canal followed the river, it often crossed the course of a creek or a stream flowing into the river. Each stream had to be conducted under the canal so that it could join the river without interfering with the canal. Small streams were conducted under the canal in low culverts built of brick or stone; they looked like sewer pipes. Across larger streams and rivers it was necessary to carry the canal on a bridge called an aqueduct. Horne designed an aqueduct to carry the Pocosink Canal over the Beaverdam River where it joined the Pocosink River. Five giant stone arches were needed to carry the heavy load of canal and towpath.

Stone piers were built on foundations that reached down to the bedrock. Thirty-five feet above the river, temporary centering was supported on the piers; these wooden forms held the stones of each arch in place until the final keystone was fitted into the top of the arch. When all of the arches were complete and the spaces between them were filled with stone, the centering was taken down. The rest of the work was like building an ordinary canal between stone walls, except it was 50 feet above the Beaverdam River.

ARCH

CENTERING

PIER

A CULVERT

By 1822 the Pocosink Canal was completed from Columbia to Third Mountain. Here the river swept in a great bend around the third of many ridges that blocked the western horizon. During Horne and Warren's 1817 survey of the canal route, they discovered coal near the top of Third Mountain. The partners realized that the canal would make it easy to ship coal from Third Mountain to the coastal cities. They also realized that a growing coal trade would ensure the success of their canal since they could collect a toll for each load of coal shipped.

To make sure of the coal trade, Warren and Horne bought 2,000 acres of land where coal was found. They formed the Pocosink Coal Company and began developing the mines and shipping docks required to get the coal out of the ground and on to the market.

At the base of the mountain, they established the town of Mount Carbon. Warren wanted the town to be a model industrial community like the ones he had read about in utopian pamphlets. He laid out streets and lots, and left space for public parks. He built a meeting house for religious services, a school, a hotel for visitors and single men, and a library and municipal hall, which he grandly named the Mount Carbon Atheneum. There was nothing like it west of First Mountain.

To get coal down the mountain from the mines, the partners decided to build a railroad. Warren surveyed a route that coal-laden railcars could descend, propelled by the force of gravity. Another railroad was built to haul empty railcars back up the mountain; it would be powered by a steam engine brought all the way from England.

The railroad was ready to be tested in August 1823. A train of six fully loaded cars rolled down the mountain. A brakeman on the first car controlled their speed so that they wouldn't fly off the rails on a curve. At the bottom, a slight upgrade helped stop the cars at the loading dock. The cars were tipped one at a time into coal bins. Coal boats were filled from the bins, weighed in a special lock to compute the toll, and towed into the canal by a team of two mules.

Empty railcars rolled on to the foot of the return track. It ran straight up the side of the mountain to an engine house at the top. A steam engine pulled the empty cars up the inclined railroad with a cable. The engine wound the cable around a great drum.

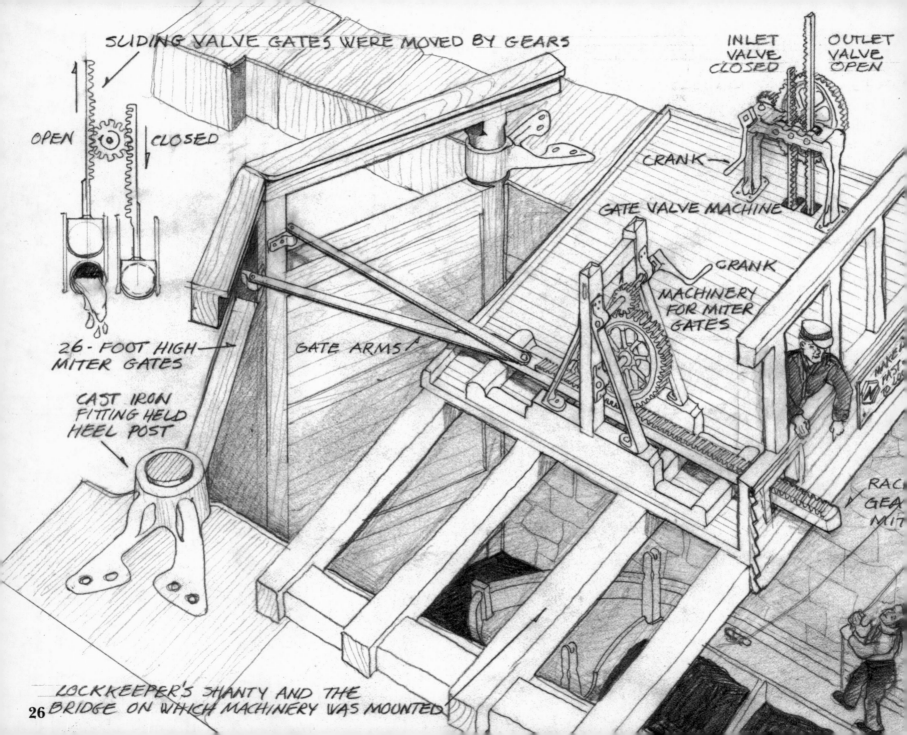

SLIDING VALVE GATES WERE MOVED BY GEARS

OPEN   CLOSED

INLET VALVE CLOSED

OUTLET VALVE OPEN

CRANK

GATE VALVE MACHINE

CRANK

MACHINERY FOR MITER GATES

26-FOOT HIGH MITER GATES

GATE ARMS

CAST IRON FITTING HELD HEEL POST

RAC GEA MIT

LOCKKEEPER'S SHANTY AND THE BRIDGE ON WHICH MACHINERY WAS MOUNTED

PINION
ED THE
TES

At the top of the incline, empty cars were reunited into six-car trains and sent to the mine, where they would be filled with coal and sent down the gravity railroad again.

Horne and Warren continued to work on the canal while construction at Mount Carbon proceeded. The coal trade was vital to the Navigation Company's finances, but the goal of reaching the Bleak River and the Ohio Valley was everything.

The most difficult barriers lay ahead. As the canal builders advanced, the valley grew narrower and the gradient, or slope, of the river grew steeper. Horne decided to build locks that would lift boats 20 feet instead of the more common 10 to 12 feet. The deeper locks would halve the number of locks needed to reach the canal's high point, and they would reduce the time required to move a boat through the locks.

The difficulties of building such locks with wood and stone were great, though. The pressure of water on the gates was tremendous; the gates must be heavier than the ones used earlier on the canal and would require machinery to be moved. The volume of water in each lock would be doubled if the depth were doubled, yet the lock should not take any longer to fill and drain if the advantages of fewer locks were to be realized. Horne devised a way of regulating the water level by using pipes and valves buried in the masonry of the locks. Water would enter each lock through pipes at each end so that the canal boats wouldn't be smashed about by the rush of water. Ironsmiths at Turtle Forge made the pipes and valves according to Horne's designs. Valves of the new design would open and close more easily under the greater water pressure than the paddle valves in the gates of the 10-foot locks.

Rack and pinion gears would allow the lockkeeper to open the inlet valve and close the outlet valve at the same time. Turning the gear in the counterdirection closed the inlet and opened the outlet when draining the lock. Another set of gears moved the heavy miter gates.

As the canal was built farther up the valley of the Pocosink, it got nearer to the river's source and higher above sea level. One final mountain separated the waters of the eastward-flowing Pocosink from the westward-flowing Bleak River. This mountain divide, or watershed, between the Pocosink Valley and the Bleak River Valley marked the greatest altitude on the route to the Bleak River and the Ohio. The divide followed the top of a long ridge called the Allegheny Mountain, some 600 feet above the Pocosink. A low place on the ridge called Nesco Gap was used by the Indians on their portages from the Pocosink River to the waters of the Ohio Valley.

Nesco Gap was the only place to cross the mountain; but how could a canal be built over such a barrier? A flight of locks that climbed the height in thirty giant steps was what Horne and Warren had boldly proposed to the company's directors. But, as they stood at Nesco Gap, the partners saw that it was impossible. Water was not available on the mountaintop in the quantities needed to operate locks; each boat's passage through a lock used 180,000 gallons. A tunnel through the mountain would be half a mile long; no one knew how to dig such a long tunnel.

When the confident partners first proposed a canal across the mountains, they were more certain of their goal than they were of the means to get there. The stockholders were not very curious about how the canal would be built, but they were certain that it must be built to bring the continent's wealth to their city. Canal building was a national craze, and what was dreamed was bound to be accomplished. So, a sense of adventure and destiny, combined with greed and boosterism, set the great enterprise in motion. It was up to Horne and Warren to find the ingenuity and determination to keep it going. Theirs was the key contribution.

The only way across the Nesco Gap was to drag the canal boats up one side of the mountain and down the other. Horne considered how it might be done. He decided that a fully loaded canal boat about half the size of the standard boat could be carried by rail over the divide. The 90-foot-long boats would have to be built in two 45-foot sections that could be taken apart and hauled up the inclined railroad one at a time. Steam engines much bigger than any yet built in North America would be needed at the summit of Nesco Gap to do the work.

Horne returned to Columbia and consulted the engineers at the Gage and Whistle Foundry and Engine Works. Horne wanted four engines, two that would pull boats up the eastern side of the mountain, and two that would pull boats up the western slope. After much study and discussion, Gage and Whistle agreed they could build the engines that met Horne's requirements. They would finish the engines and the related machinery in a year and a half.

Horne and Warren completed their plans for the inclined railways. They ordered iron rails and hardware from Turtle Forge, and sent woodsmen out to cut the timbers that would be needed when construction began the next year.

As Horne approached Nesco Gap in March, 1828, the mountainside looked like an anthill from the distance. Man and animals were working to shape a broad, straight ramp up the mountain. At the summit, Nesco Gap was cut down 20 feet to make a platform for engine houses. Halfway to the summit, the ramp was broken by a level place where an engine house would also stand. When the ramp was finished, the workmen laid oak rails 5 feet apart on oak or pine crossties, timbers which were notched to hold the rails. The crossties were laid upon a bed of broken stone. Iron bands were spiked to the top of the rails, where the wheels would run. Two such railways were built parallel to one another up the eastern slope; one track for cars to descend to the Pocosink, the other track for cars to be pulled up to the summit. A similar railway was built on the western slope of Nesco Gap. Each inclined plane would have its own engine to pull a continuous loop of rope up one track and down the other track. Railcars tied to this rope would carry canal boats up and down the portage.

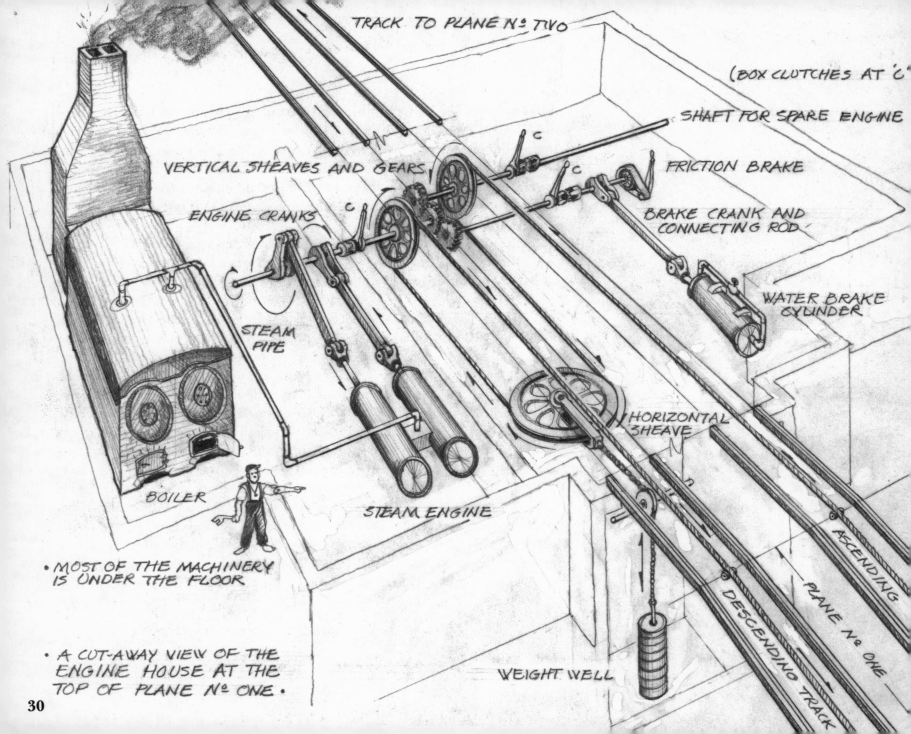

TRACK TO PLANE Nº TWO

(BOX CLUTCHES AT 'C')

SHAFT FOR SPARE ENGINE

VERTICAL SHEAVES AND GEARS

FRICTION BRAKE

ENGINE CRANKS

BRAKE CRANK AND
CONNECTING ROD

STEAM
PIPE

WATER BRAKE
CYLINDER

BOILER

STEAM ENGINE

HORIZONTAL
SHEAVE

ASCENDING

PLANE Nº ONE

DESCENDING TRACK

• MOST OF THE MACHINERY
IS UNDER THE FLOOR

• A CUT-AWAY VIEW OF THE
ENGINE HOUSE AT THE
TOP OF PLANE Nº ONE.

WEIGHT WELL

30

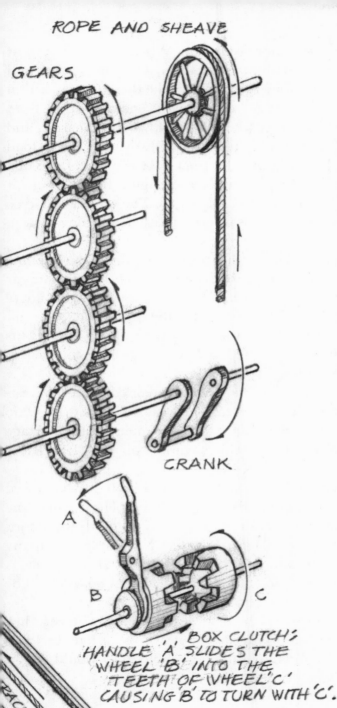

ROPE AND SHEAVE

GEARS

CRANK

A

B   C

BOX CLUTCH:
HANDLE 'A' SLIDES THE
WHEEL 'B' INTO THE
TEETH OF WHEEL 'C'
CAUSING 'B' TO TURN WITH 'C'.

The rope would be heavy, 8½ inches around, and it would pass over sheaves at the top and bottom of the inclined plane. Gage and Whistle cast the sheaves as giant iron wheels; they cut a groove to grip the rope in the rim of each wheel. Vertical sheaves connected to an engine would wind the rope. The rope would pass below the rails where a horizontal sheave would keep it tight. The machinery at the foot of the plane was similar, except the vertical sheaves were not powered.

The horizontal sheaves on the inclined railroad were loaded with tons of iron to keep the rope tight. The hemp ropes were over a mile long and weighed about 13,000 pounds. Changes in air moisture would affect the rope's length, or a heavy canal boat would stretch it. Horne's machinery allowed for these changes and would keep the cars moving on the railroad.

By midsummer of the next year everything was ready for the steam engines. But Gage and Whistle were not satisfied with the performance of their engines and asked Horne to allow three more months to work on them. Horne agreed; he preferred that improvements be made at the foundry rather than on the mountaintop. He realized that the steam engine was a sort of practical experiment; results came as much from trial and error as by design.

In 1830 the completed engines lay in Gage and Whistle Company's yard surrounded by gears, brake assemblies, and sheaves. Each engine was put on a canal boat; the other parts filled two more boats. Mr. Whistle and four mechanics followed the engines to Nesco Gap, where they would assemble the machinery and prove its worthiness.

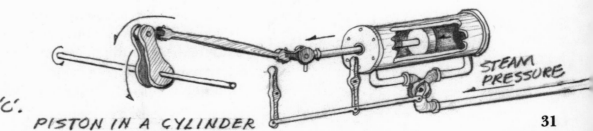

PISTON IN A CYLINDER

STEAM PRESSURE

The engines were fired with coal from Mount Carbon. When a boat arrived at the foot of the eastern inclined railroad, its two sections were uncoupled and floated onto cars run into the water on submerged rails. While the boat was tied in place, the workers fastened the car to the heavy rope. Now the engineer at the head of the plane started the machinery. The great wheels turned, wound the rope, and pulled the car and boat out of the water and up the steep railway. The heavy load was balanced by a boat descending on the parallel tracks. At the top of the first inclined plane, the car reached a level track inside the engine house where it stopped and was hitched to the rope on plane number two. The engine at Nesco summit pulled car and boat up the second plane; there was no descending boat so the engine worked harder.

When the car reached the summit, it was pushed to the engine house at plane number three. Here, the car tenders hitched the rope to the rear of the car. The car would roll down the mountain powered by its weight. A brake in the engine house controlled the speed of the turning sheaves and the rate of the canal boat's descent.

At the foot of plane number four, the boat was floated free of the railcars, its sections were reunited, and its towline was hitched to a fresh mule team for the trip down the canal.

The western, or Bleak River, division of the canal was extended from the western inclined railroad to the place where the Bleak River flowed into the Ohio River. While Ezra Horne labored with mechanics and workmen on the portage railroad, Joshua Warren and crews of canal builders worked on the Bleak River division.

The first boat to cross the portage railroad at Nesco Gap in 1830 was towed along the canal to its terminus at the mouth of the Bleak River. Here, where the booming river town of Ohiopolis grew around the remains of an old trading fort, was the goal of the entire canal scheme; it took the Pocosink Navigation Company twelve years to reach it. Ohiopolis was opposite the mouth of the Bleak River. A cable was rigged across the Ohio River so the unmanageable canal boats could be brought over the turbulent water.

A gang of rivermen would climb on board the boat at the canal entrance. They would tie the boat to pulleys on the cable. With the aid of sweeps, or long paddles, and by hauling the boat hand-over-hand along the taut cable, they would take it to the safety of the Ohiopolis shore.

EAR RIVER -
VISION

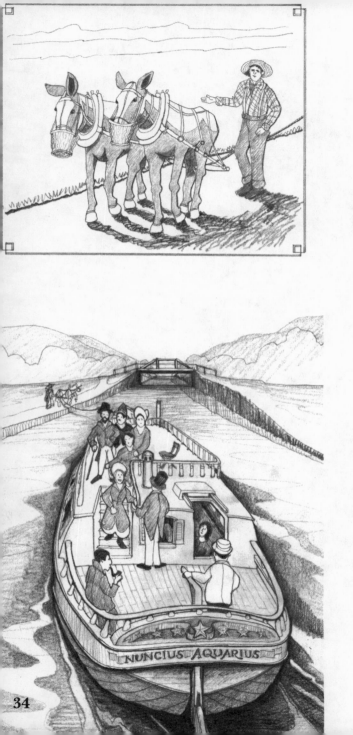

A trip on the Pocosink Navigation route from Columbia to Ohiopolis took twelve days in 1842. The canal had been operating for twelve years, and a number of companies ran packet boats that carried passengers, mail, and parcels on regular schedules. The boat *Nuncius Aquarius* of the Astral Packet Line was the newest packet on the canal. It left Columbia at seven o'clock in the morning, after the passengers ate breakfast.

A matched pair of mules trudged along the towpath at the pace of a quick walk; they pulled on a long rope fastened to the towing post in the bow of the packet boat. The mule driver walked beside the team. The captain stood in the stern of the boat and guided it with deft pressure on the tiller—a sort of lever that moved the rudder and steered the boat. A sudden or extreme movement of the tiller might bump the boat into the bank and shake up the passengers, so the captain had to keep a sharp lookout for bends in the canal, oncoming boats, and the mule's movements.

Fair weather brought most of the passengers out of the cabin onto the narrow deck. Some climbed on the roof, where folding chairs were set up. The view was good from this vantage, but when the boat approached a bridge, everyone scrambled down to avoid being knocked off. Bridges were only high enough to clear the cabin roof. Some passengers jumped from the moving boat to the bank for a brisk walk along the towpath with the driver and mule team.

When the packet boat caught up with a slower freight boat, the captain blew on a brass horn to signal the freight boat. The slower boat's mule team was stopped, allowing the towrope to slacken as the overtaken boat drifted on, steered toward the far bank. The packet boat was towed without a pause past the overtaken boat, gliding over its sunken towrope.

The packet's passengers stared at the freighter and its crew. The boat was owned by the Pocosink Navigation Company. It was a standard sectional boat built in two parts that were fastened together for canal travel but could be unhooked and taken separately over the portage railroad.

The crew on this boat was a family. The captain drove the mules; his wife stood at the tiller. Their two children played on the cabin roof. The younger was harnessed and tied to the cabin so he wouldn't be lost overboard. The whole family lived in a tiny cabin at the stern of the boat. Space was so tight, it was no wonder that most of the captains were bachelors or, if they married, left their families ashore. A few of the boats were captained by women who had grown up on the canal and loved the boating life.

The *Nuncius Aquarius* approached Little Falls locks. Passengers found the process of "locking through" a welcome break from the confinement of the boat. They could step ashore, stretch their legs, and observe the locking operations. It took most of an hour to get through the four locks at Little Falls, so there was time to sketch or talk to the lockkeeper's children and pet his dog. The locks were operated from six o'clock in the morning until eight in the evening, six days a week.

On Sundays, when the canal was shut down, the packet boats usually anchored near a town so that their passengers could spend the day on shore. Other boats lay by for a day of rest wherever they found themselves. The children might go to church if they were near one; more likely, they would find themselves on a quiet bend in the canal with nothing to do but fish or swim. For this reason, the ladies on the packet didn't consider canal boats very suitable for raising children. Canal boaters had a close community in spite of their always being on the move. Everyone on the canal knew each other, and their children usually found work on the canal when they grew up.

As the *Nuncius Aquarius* passed Mount Carbon, the busy coal docks came into view. Mount Carbon was a thriving town in 1842. It was the county seat and the headquarters of the Pocosink Navigation Company, whose offices occupied a fine new building facing the canal.

Coal cars filled the narrow valley with their racket when a train rumbled down the gravity railroad from the mines. Every working day was punctuated by the sound of coal on its way to market. But most people cheerfully accepted as signs of prosperity the noise and dust that intruded on this former wilderness.

Beyond Mount Carbon, the *Nuncius Aquarius* climbed a series of 20-foot locks and passed along an especially scenic part of the canal. Passengers spent all day gazing at the landscape and murmuring about its sublime beauty. They named every rock, mountain, and feature. Here was the Indian Head or Pompey's Nose; there was the Hermit Cave. Travel by canal was fun; it was a leisurely glide through a changing landscape, and it was the last word in transportation.

Most of the boats on the canal carried not passengers but freight. The turning basin at the foot of the Nesco Portage Railroad was a good place to look at the variety of boats on the canal. The turning basin was a man-made pond big enough to hold twenty or more boats as they awaited their turn on the inclined railroad or as they unloaded their cargo into smaller boats if they were too big for the portage.

Canal boats had to fit the locks on the Pocosink; they could not be longer than 90 feet, wider than 10½ feet, or deeper than 5 feet. Most boats were built to those dimensions, but they could be smaller.

Boat design varied. There were square-ended, scowlike boats to haul stone, sand, and iron ore. There were also the more graceful boats with rounded ends of the Pocosink Coal Company. There were the many sectional boats built to cross the Nesco Portage, and there were packet boats to carry passengers. Packet boats like the *Nuncius Aquarius* had the sleekest and most graceful shape; even though they followed a pair of mules, they looked as if they could fly.

The Pocosink Navigation Company had several boats built for its purposes. Inspection boats carried company officials and engineers on their business. Repair boats were equipped to maintain the canal banks, locks, and bridges. A sudden storm might wash out part of the earth bank and drain the canal. Quick action was needed to stop the flow of water and earth, so repair boats and their crews were stationed at regular intervals along the canal.

The *Nuncius Aquarius* took its turn on the Nesco Portage Railroad. Passengers rode to the summit in a special railcar while the packet was taken apart. One section was loaded on a railcar and hauled up the inclined railroad; the other section followed. At the top they were put on the western inclined railroad and lowered to the Bleak River. Passengers sat on the veranda of a small tearoom to watch the activity on the portage railroad; they rode down the western incline to board their boat when it was ready.

The voyage along the Bleak River division of the Pocosink Canal took four days. Packet companies hired fresh mules every day when they could. Packet drivers kept their teams to a pace of 20 miles per day; mules pulling heavy cargo boats traveled about 15 miles per day. Cargo boats didn't keep to a schedule, and their captains and drivers were responsible for their animals. Canal boaters judged one another by the care they took of their mules and were proud of a healthy, well-matched pair. Mules often ate from feed bags as they walked; they stopped whenever they needed water, and they frequently wore hats to shade their heads, or tasseled coats to ward off biting flies. A good team worked twenty years on the canal before retiring.

At the junction of the Bleak River with the Ohio, the last lock on the canal let the packet boat out into the river. Mules were led to a paddock where they ate and rested. The packet was tied to a cable stretched across the Ohio River and pulled to the busy town of Ohiopolis. The cable held the boat against the force of the moving river. The cable was often snagged by trees floating downriver, and it also interfered with the long timber rafts that came the same way. The Pocosink Navigation Company wanted to avoid the damage caused by snags, and the claims paid to raftsmen. An aqueduct to carry the Pocosink Canal above the Ohio directly to Ohiopolis was the solution, but a very difficult and expensive one. The Ohio was wider and deeper than the Pocosink or Bleak rivers; a stone arch aqueduct was too difficult and expensive to consider.

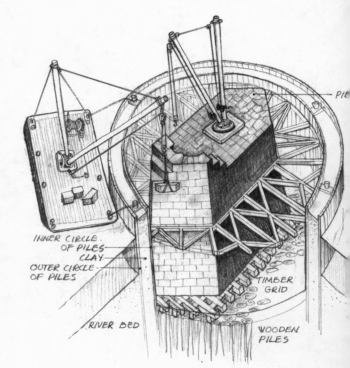

INNER CIRCLE OF PILES

CLAY

OUTER CIRCLE OF PILES

PILE

TIMBER GRID

RIVER BED

WOODEN PILES

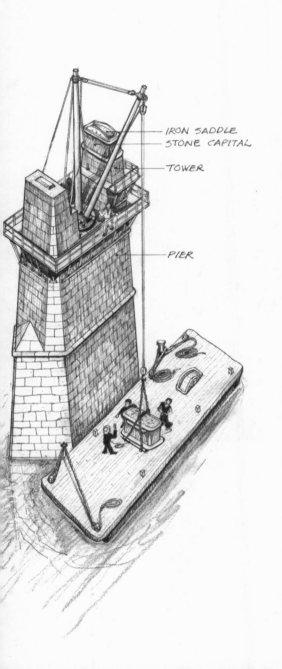

IRON SADDLE
STONE CAPITAL

TOWER

PIER

After two canal boats were torn from the cable by a timber raft that got out of control in 1844, the company decided to attempt a new way of carrying the canal over the Ohio, by suspending it from wire cables. The idea was proposed by John Ropewalk, an inventor and manufacturer of the new cables that were serving so well on the Nesco Portage Railroad. Horne, who once owned a wire factory in Columbia, saw the advantages of Ropewalk's design over any stone or timber structure. Horne campaigned to get the company's directors to agree. They respected Horne's judgment and accepted the proposal once they understood the design.

The suspension aqueduct at Ohiopolis was begun in 1844. It would be carried on stone piers 190 feet apart; this distance between supports established a span. Seven spans of 190 feet each would bridge the Ohio.

To make a pier, the builders drove a circle of wooden piles into the bed of the river. Piles are long tree trunks, upended and pounded into the ground. A larger circle was driven around the first, and the space between them was packed with clay to make a watertight cofferdam in midstream. Pumps run by a waterwheel drained the cofferdam until workmen could see the bottom. Workers then dug through the soft mud on the river bottom to more solid earth. From that level they drove clusters of piles deeper. The piles were cut even, and a timber grid was laid across them; spaces were filled with stone and mortar. On this platform the heavy stone piers were built. When the masons had built the piers above river level, the cofferdams were removed. The piers were all the same height, 42 feet above low water. A pair of stone towers was built on each pier to a height of 60 feet. Next, the towers were capped with iron castings shaped like saddles; they would support the wrought-iron cables hanging across all eight towers. Cable ends were fastened at four massive anchorages, two at each end of the bridge. The weight of the stone abutments would hold the cables against the load of the entire bridge. The cables would be 10½ inches thick, made up of 3,220 wires.

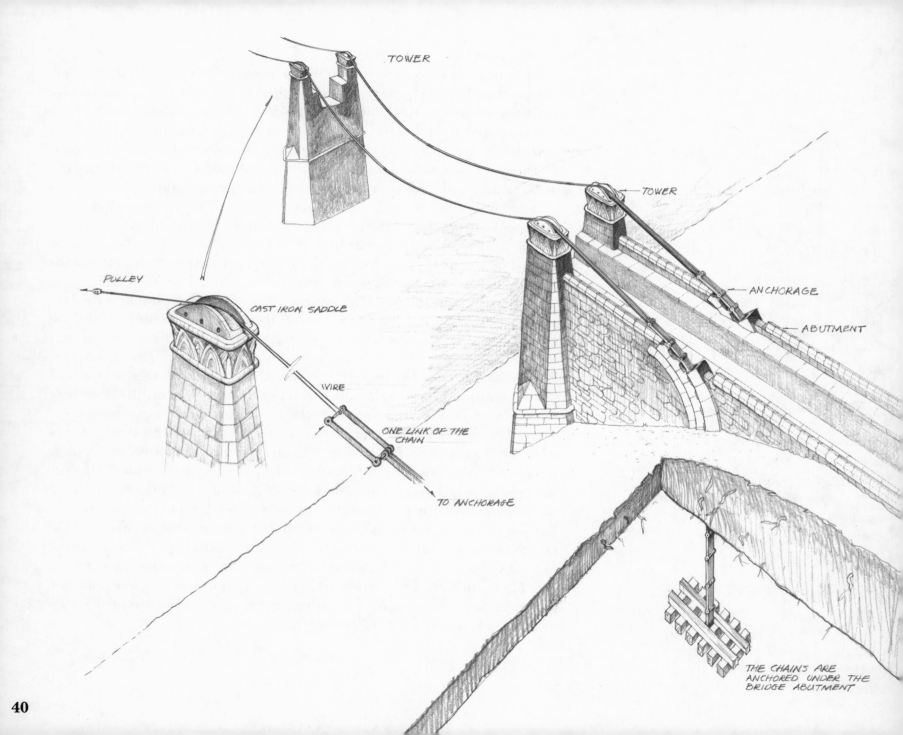

TOWER

TOWER

PULLEY

CAST IRON SADDLE

ANCHORAGE

ABUTMENT

WIRE

ONE LINK OF THE
CHAIN

TO ANCHORAGE

THE CHAINS ARE
ANCHORED UNDER THE
BRIDGE ABUTMENT

40

A DETAIL SHOWING HOW THE SEVEN BUNDLES OF WIRE WERE PACKED INTO A 10½" CABLE.

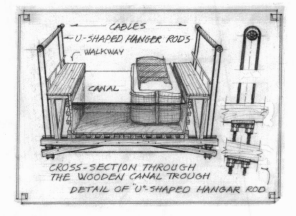

CABLES
U-SHAPED HANGER RODS
WALKWAY
CANAL

CROSS-SECTION THROUGH THE WOODEN CANAL TROUGH
DETAIL OF "U"-SHAPED HANGAR ROD

IRON SADDLE

CABLE
HANGER ROD

TIMBERS TO CARRY THE CANAL TROUGH

Ropewalk had a traveling pulley rigged across the tops of the towers; it was used to pull the wire across the river from the Bleak River anchorage to the Ohiopolis anchorage. The wire was looped through the end of a giant chain. Seven heavy chains were anchored deep in the masonry of each stone abutment to resist the pull on the wires.

The wire lay on the iron saddle atop each tower and hung in graceful curves from tower to tower. Cable was built up by pulling additional wires across the river to hang in the same curve. The pulley would return to the Bleak River shore and carry two more strands of wire across the river; it took 1,610 trips to spin the wires for one cable. The wires were gathered into seven bundles of 460 wires each. Between the towers the bundles were packed into a round shape, varnished, and wrapped for protection from weather. When two thick cables hung across the river from tower to tower in uniform curves, the cables were ready for hanging the aqueduct.

Pairs of wrought-iron rods were bent into U shapes and hung upside down over the cables. Timbers were hung between pairs of hanger rods; the timbers supported a canal trough. The canal trough was a big wooden box whose sides and bottom were watertight; it would hold 6 feet of water. The entire load of the canal was suspended from iron rods hung from wire cables slung between stone towers, a beautiful and daring structure. The timber aqueduct also carried a walkway on each side of the trough; the walkways helped stiffen the sides against water pressure.

When the aqueduct was finished, it was linked to a turning basin in Ohiopolis and to the canal along the Bleak River. The water surface in the aqueduct was 48 feet above low water in the Ohio River. The last four locks that formerly lowered boats to river level were eliminated when the canal was connected to the aqueduct.

Crowds from Ohiopolis and the countryside flocked to the inauguration of the aqueduct in 1848. Throngs of rubbernecking backwoodsmen were astounded by the sight of a 140-ton canal boat gliding 48 feet above the mighty Ohio. The Pocosink Navigation Company had truly reached the terminus at Ohiopolis proposed by Horne and Warren thirty years before.

The thirtieth anniversary of the Pocosink Navigation Company also marked the end of its monopoly on transportation in the Pocosink Valley. In 1848 the first train of the Columbia and Western Railroad arrived at Mount Carbon from Columbia. Railroads hardly existed when the canal was started in 1818. Improvements in steam engines, the same improvements that enabled steam to pull loaded canal boats up the Nesco Gap inclined railroad, eventually made it possible to put on wheels an engine powerful enough to pull a train of railcars. During the 1830s railroads were built from a few cities into the hinterlands. The locomotive engines couldn't climb any but the slightest grades, so they were no threat to canals. In the 1840s better locomotives were built, and rails extended deeper into the countryside. It wouldn't be long before the Columbia and Western, or some other railroad, reached Ohiopolis from the seaboard.

Railroads could be built more cheaply and more quickly than canals. They operated year-round, while most canals were closed by ice in winter. Trains traveled much faster than the leisurely pace of the mule team on the towpath. It was only a matter of time before the railroad would replace the canal; the directors of the Pocosink Navigation Company recognized this fact. Although the canal could still carry heavy things like coal, iron, and timber great distances more cheaply than a railroad, railroads could more easily carry passengers, parcels, and perishable goods. The directors decided to make improvements in their canal where it could compete for the heavy freight and bulk cargo traffic, and where the costs of operating the canal could be cut. Where heavy traffic was delayed by locks, parallel locks were built to permit upward and downward traffic at the same time.

When the Columbia and Western Railroad crossed the mountains to Ohiopolis in 1854, passenger travel on the Pocosink Navigation route fell off noticeably. Ten years later the Pocosink Navigation Company sold the Bleak River division to the railroad. The steam engines on Nesco Gap were stilled, and the great aqueduct at Ohiopolis was converted to a railroad bridge, bringing the Columbia and Western into a new terminal at the center of the city.

When a great flood in 1872 wrecked several locks on the canal above Mount Carbon, the company was slow to rebuild them. The financial panic of 1873 caused an economic depression that obliged the directors to sell off everything but the canal from Mount Carbon to Columbia. The coal and navigation companies were combined in the same year, and the waterway was used almost exclusively to ship coal. The integration of the coal-mining, transportation, and marketing operations made the business profitable until the financial panic of 1929. The canal was abandoned in 1932 after more than one hundred years of service.

Many of the stone locks still stand amid weeds and trees. Horne's work was intended to last forever; the Pocosink Navigation Company lived for only a century. You can still find the remains of the canal if you leave the highway, cross the rail tracks, and go down by the river.

Remains of the early nineteenth-century canals can be found throughout eastern North America. There are almost fifty sites where a canal, lock, dam, or other structure has been uncovered and preserved. Some sites provide exhibits that explain how the canal came to be there, or show how people lived and worked in the age of canal travel. Here are twenty of the most informative exhibits:

Illinois
Illinois and Michigan Canal Museum, Old Canal Town Historical District, Lockport, Ill.

Indiana
Whitewater Canal, Metamora, Ind.

Maryland
Chesapeake and Ohio Canal National Historical Park extends 184 miles from Cumberland, Md. to Georgetown in Washington, D.C. A museum at Great Falls Tavern, Md. tells the story of the canal.

Chesapeake and Delaware Canal Museum, Chesapeake City, Md.

Massachusetts
Lowell National Historical Park, Lowell, Mass., traces the role of water power and canal transportation in the growth of industry along the Merrimack River Canal.

Middlesex Canal, Woburn, Mass.

New Jersey
Waterloo Village is on the Morris Canal, near Netcong, N.J. A series of exhibits in a museum village is presented by the Waterloo Village Foundation and the New Jersey Canal Society Museum.

Delaware and Raritan Canal State Park has a fully watered canal stretching from Lambertville to Perth Amboy, N.J.

New York
Erie Canal Village, Rome, N.Y.

Erie Canal Museum, Syracuse, N.Y., tells the story of North America's greatest canal.

Delaware and Hudson Canal Museum, High Falls, N.Y., tells the history of a canal built to ship coal.

Ohio
Roscoe Village, Coshockton, Ohio, is on the Ohio and Erie Canal.

Canal Fulton, Ohio, is also on the Ohio and Erie Canal.

Piqua Historical Area, Piqua, Ohio, is on the Miami and Erie Canal.

Ontario
Bytown Museum, Ottawa, is at the entrance to the Rideau Waterway whose 123 miles of navigation and forty-seven locks are almost exactly as they were built.

Pennsylvania
Delaware and Hudson Canal Aqueduct, Lackawaxen, Pa., is preserved as a national historical landmark. The suspension aqueduct was built by the famous engineer John Roebling.

Canal Museum and Hugh Moore Park, Easton, Pa., presents the history of the Lehigh Navigation and the connecting Morris Canal and Delaware Division Canal.

Union Canal Tunnel Park near Lebanon, Pa. Restored locks and a visitor's center preserve more of the Union Canal at the nearby Tulpehocken Creek Valley Park.

Port Clinton Canal Museum, Port Clinton, Pa., presents the history of the Schuylkill Navigation.

Allegheny Portage Railroad National Historical Site near Cresson, Pa., marks the summit level of the first canal and railroad system to cross the Allegheny Front.

aqueduct: A bridge that supports a canal.

balance beam: The timber on a miter gate used to move the gate.

barometer: An instrument that determines air pressure.

bypass flume: An artificial channel that conducts water past a gate or barrier.

clutch: A device for coupling two shafts so they will turn together.

cofferdam: An enclosure to divert water from the bed of a stream to permit construction.

compass: An instrument with a magnetic needle which determines magnetic north.

culvert: An arched drain under a road or canal.

cylinder: A closed tube in which a piston moves back and forth.

engineer: A designer or builder of machinery.

fall line: The boundary between low, coastal lands and higher, rocky lands, marked by falls or rapids, beyond which boats cannot travel.

gate valve: A sliding door that regulates the flow of water.

gear: A toothed wheel which transfers motion from or to a shaft.

grade: The steepness of a slope, expressed as the vertical distance divided by the horizontal distance.

guard lock: A lock that protects the canal from floods.

hanger rod: The U-shaped rod that hangs over a cable on a suspension aqueduct.

heel post: The wooden post on which a miter gate turns.

hemp: An herb (*Cannabis sativa*) whose tough fibers make strong rope.

level: A surveying instrument that determines a horizontal plane.

leveling rod: A stick used by a surveying team for measuring heights.

lock: An enclosure in a canal with gates at each end, used to raise and lower boats.

miter gates: A pair of swinging gates used in a lock that meet at an angle, or miter, so that they will stay closed against water pressure.

paddle valve: A paddle-like door in a lock gate that regulates the flow of water.

pile: A long pole or plank driven into the earth.

piston: A short rod that slides within a hollow cylinder.

plane table: A drawing board, mounted on a tripod, that is set up over a point on a map from which other points are mapped.

portage: The carrying of boats and goods over land between navigable waters; also the route over which boats and goods are carried.

pulley: One or more sheaves within a block, used to change the direction of or increase the power on a rope.

rack and pinion: A gear whereby a toothed bar (a rack) is moved back and forth as a pinion (a toothed wheel) is turned.

shaft: A bar used to transmit the turning motion of wheels and gears.

sheave: A grooved wheel, around which a rope is pulled.

slack water: Water that doesn't move; still water.

surveyor: One who determines the dimensions and position of a geographical area.

tidal lock: A lock that moves boats to the changing level of the sea.

toll: A fee charged for the use of a canal or other means of transportation.

towline: A rope used to pull a boat.

towpath: A path along the canal used by the mules or horses that pulled the boats.

tow post: A post fixed near the bow, or front end, of a boat to which the towline is tied.

valve: A device to stop or regulate a flow of water.

water brake: A device to slow or stop motion by applying the resistance of water.

watershed: A divide between one drainage area or basin and another.

waterwheel: A wheel that turns by the action of flowing water.

weir: A small dam that regulates the level or flow of water.

INDEX

Albany (New York), 3
Allegheny Mountain, 10, 28
Anchorages, 39, *40,* 41
Aqueducts, 10, 22, *22–23,* 38–43, 47
Arches, 22, *23*
Astral Packet Line, 34

Balance beam, *14,* 18, 47
Barometer, 9, 47
Beaverdam River, 11, 22
Beulah Gap, 10
Bleak River, 8–10, 27, 28, 32, 38, 41, 44
Boat captains, 34, 35, 38
Boat crews, 35
Brake, 31, *31*
Bridges, 34, 36, 39
Buffalo (New York), 3
Bypass flume, *13,* 15, 47

Cables, 25, 32, 38, 39, 41
Canal bank, 17, 34, 36
Canal boats, 18, 25, 27–29, 31–32, 34–39, 43, 44
Canal trough, 41
Canoes, *6,* 7
Cargo, 36, 38
Cargo boats, 34, 36, 38
Channels, 8
Charter, 9
Children on boats, 35
Clutch, *31,* 47
Coal trade, 25, 27, 35, 36, 44, 45
Cofferdams, 12, *12,* 39, 47
Columbia, 9, 11, 12, 15, 17, 25, 29, 34, 39, 44, 45
Columbia and Western Railroad, 44
Commerce, 3, 5, 7–9, 25, 27, 35–36, 38, 44, 45
Compass, 9, 47
Culvert, 22, *22,* 47
Cylinder, *31,* 47

Dams, 8, 12, *13,* 15, 17, 39, 47

Engine house, 25, *30, 31,* 32
Engineers, 8, 29, 32, 47
Erie Canal, 3
Europe, 8

Fall line, *4, 5,* 5, 7, *11,* 47
First Mountain, 11, 25
Flight (locks), 15
Floods, 17, 45

Gage and Whistle Foundry and Engine Works, 29, 31
Gate, 18, 21, *26,* 27
Gate valve, *26,* 47

Gear, *26,* 27, *30,* 31, *31,* 47
Grade (gradient), 27, 47
Guard lock, *13,* 17, 47

Hanger rod, 41, *41,* 47
Heel post, *14, 15,* 15, *26,* 47
Hemp rope, 31, 47
Horne, Ezra, 8, 9, 12, 15, 20, 21, 25, 27–29, 31, 32, 39, 43, 45
Hudson River, 3

Inclined railroad, 28–29, 31–32, *32, 33,* 36, 38, 39, 44
Indians, 7, 28
Inlet valve, *26,* 27
Inspection boats, 36
Iron saddle, 39, *39, 40, 41*

Lake Erie, 3
Level, 9, 47
Leveling rod, 9, 47
Little Falls, 11–13, 15, 17, 18, 35
Little Falls dam, 12, 15, 17, 20
Lockkeeper, 13–15, 18, *26,* 27, 35
Locks, 13–21, 27, 28, 35, 36, 38, 43, 44, 45, 47
Locomotives, 44

Miter, *15*
Miter gates, *14,* 15, *15,* 17, *26–27,* 27, 47
Mohawk River, 3
Mount Carbon, 11, 25, 32, 35, 36, 44, 45
Mount Carbon Atheneum, 25, 27
Mountain crossing, 28–33
Mule driver, *19,* 34, 35, 38
Mules, 5, 17, *19,* 20, 25, 32, 34–36, 38, 44

Navigation, 3, 9–11, 20, 27
Nesco Gap, 10, 28, 29, 31, 32, 44
Nesco Portage Railroad, 36, 38, 39
Nuncius Aquarius (boat), 34, *34,* 35, 36, 38

Ohio River, 9, 10, 19, 28, 32, 38, 39, 43
Ohio River Valley, 8, 9, 27, 28
Ohiopolis, *10,* 32, 34, 38, 39, 41, 43, 44
Outlet valve, *26,* 27
Overflow weir, 13, 47

Packet boats, 34, 35, 38
Paddle valves, *14,* 15, 18, 27, 47
Passengers, 34–36, 38, 44
Piers, 22, *23,* 38, 39, *39*
Piles (wood), *38,* 39, 47
Piston, *31,* 47
Plane, 29–32
Plane table, 9, 47
Pocosink Coal Company, 25, 36
Pocosink Navigation Company, 3, 8, 9, 27, 32, 34–36, 38, 39, 43–45
Pocosink River, 8–12, 17, 20, 22, 28, 29, 38

Pocosink Valley, 9, 28, 44
Port cities, 5
Portage, 7, 8, 10, 29, 34, 36, 38, 47
Pulleys, 32, 41, 47

Rack and pinion gears, *26–27,* 27, 47
Rafts, 38, 39
Railroad, 25, 27–36, 38, 44, *44–45*
Rapids, 5, 7, 8, 11, 12
Repair boats, 36
Ropewalk, John, 39, 41
Ruins, 3, 45, 46

Sectional boats, 28, 32, 34, 36, 38
Settlers, 8
Shaft, *30,* 47
Sheaves, *30,* 31, *31,* 32, 47
Shipping docks, 25
Slack water, 13, 20, 47
Span, 39
Steam engine, 25, 28, *30,* 31, 32, 44
Stone abutments, 39, 41
Stone locks, 45
Stone towers, 39–41
Stop timbers, 17
Streams, 22
Surveying, 8, 9, *9,* 12, 21 25, .47
Suspension acqueduct, 39
Sweeps (long paddles), 32

Temporary centering, 22, *23*
Third Mountain, 10, 11, 25
Tidal lock, 17, 47
Tiller, 34, 35
Toll, 9, 15, 25, 47
Towline, 32, 34, 47
Towpath, 11, *13,* 17, 20, 22, 34, 44, 47
Tow post, 34, 47
Turning basin, 36, 43
Turtle Forge, 11, 20, 21, 27, 29

Valves, 18, *26,* 27, 47

Warren, Joshua, 8, 9, 12, 20, 21, 25, 27–29, 32, 43
Water brake, *30,* 47
Water level, 15, 17, 18, 27
Water pressure, 15, 27, 41
Watershed, 28, 47
Waterwheels, 9, 39, 47
Weight well, *30*
Weir, *13,* 17, 47
Western settlements, 8
Women captains, 35